BONSAI

THE PRACTICAL GUIDE TO CULTIVATING & GROWING LIVING ART

DAICHI HARUKA
THE BROTHERS GREEN

ADMORE PUBLISHING

© Copyright 2019 - All rights reserved Admore Publishing

ISBN: 9781085930505

ISBN: 978-3-96772-006-8

The content contained within this book may not be reproduced, duplicated or transmitted without direct written permission from the author or the publisher.

Under no circumstances will any blame or legal responsibility be held against the publisher, or author, for any damages, reparation, or monetary loss due to the information contained within this book. Either directly or indirectly.

Cover Design by Rihan W. Cover artwork by wallpapersafari.com

Icons used for chapter headings are made by Freepik from www.flaticon.com

Published by Admore Publishing: Roßbachstraße, Berlin, Germany

Printed in the United States of America

www.publishing.admore-marketing.com

CONTENTS

Foreword — v
Introduction — ix

1. History — 1
2. Bonsai Styles — 9
3. Indoor or Outdoor — 25
4. Tool Box — 31
5. Grow from seeds or Buy a tree? — 37
6. Tree Species — 41
7. What to Look for in a Tree — 51
8. Planting a tree in a Pot — 57
9. Pruning and Trimming — 63
10. Wiring — 69
11. When to Wire — 77
12. Watering & Fertilizing — 83
13. Repotting — 87
14. Seasonal Care — 93
15. Displaying Your Bonsai — 99
16. Tips & Ideas! — 103

Afterword — 109
Thank You — 111
Resources Page — 113

FOREWORD

Hi, my name is Daichi and I'm a member of The Brothers Green.

We are a group of friends (read - "green thumbs") who love all things horticulture. Our purpose is to help others in all aspects of growing, pruning... and well, just plain old gardening!

Out of our little group I am the expert in all things Bonsai.

You may have grabbed this book because you are interested in finding out more about the hobby.

Perhaps you are looking for specific guidance on *shaping* a tree you already own...

... Or you are simply an enthusiast with years of experience and you want some extra tips to further refine your skills.

Whatever the reason, **I want to thank you for reading and checking out this book.**

This book is dedicated entirely to teaching you all I know about Bonsai. In it you will learn about everything from the history of the art to wiring and shaping techniques. Read on for straight to the point information and plenty of tips and tricks.

❝
I feel a great regard for trees; they represent age and beauty and the miracles of life and growth.

-Louise Dickinson Rich-

INTRODUCTION

ART - NATURE - CONNECTION

"Bon-sai"

Literally translated this Japanese term means "planted in a container". Bonsai however, is an art form that means much more. Derived from an ancient Chinese horticultural practice, it has continually evolved and today is a hobby enjoyed by millions around the world. The growing and sculpting of Bonsai trees is amazingly satisfying. One takes a simple sapling and molds it patiently. Then slowly with continued care you create your own unique piece of living art.

Indescribably rewarding...

The goal of Bonsai is to create the appearance of great size and age although the actual tree is small. This is possible by creating a Bonsai with strong roots that extend in all directions. This forms a solid base and allows for a sense of stability. The trunk will taper as it goes upward and features clearly defined and placed branches. A Bonsai concludes with a clear apex. It all combines to create a carefully thought out blend of symmetry, proportion and balance. Hobbyist carefully calculate every element and even the display area and pot harmonize well with the plant.

Bonsai is the art of growing trees in a confined space. Hobbyist look to simulate certain environmental conditions such as age, contorted forms, landscape, extreme weathering and other factors. Bonsai trees are shaped and inspired by nature's effects on trees, just on a reduced scale.

The shaping and manipulating of a Bonsai creates a new level of connection between nature and man. In today's fast moving world many of us have become disconnected. Cement jungles along with traffic jammed highways are our realities. Bonsais create a connection to nature that goes deeper than recreating it in a miniature tree. Working with one allows for a stronger connection. You will gain a new sense of appreciation for nature and you may start looking at trees, bushes, shrubs and life (it may sound like a stretch but this has been the case for me) differently. For some the connection turns into a form of meditation and expression.

When a Bonsai tree is cared for properly, it can live for hundreds of years. Some are passed on from generation to generation as a family heirloom. This way the original owner is always remembered and admired for their creation that lives on.

In this book, we will introduce you to the history of the art-form and introduce you to the techniques to assist you in growing your own Bonsai masterpieces. What makes this truly special is there is no "correct" way to do this. Bonsai is not an art of perfection. Every Bonsai master was once a beginner so I encourage you to enjoy the read and then the learning process... Let's get started!

❝

Our brains are like bonsai trees, growing around our private versions of reality

―Sloane Crosley―

1

HISTORY

Although the word "*Bonsai*" is Japanese, the art form originated in China. Bonsai has a long and storied history as it first appeared over a thousand years ago. By the year 700 AD the Chinese started an art known as "*pun-sai*". Pun-sai is a craft of growing single dwarf trees in pots. The trees have very little leafage and their highlights are their rugged trunks. The trunks can often look like dragons, birds or other animals. There are many myths and legends surrounding these animal-like pun-sai and this allows them to still be highly prized today.

JAPAN - KAMAKURA PERIOD (1185-1333)

Overtime, Japan adopted many of Chinas cultural elements. This was especially true during the Kamakura period (1185-1333). It was a time when Zen

Buddhism was rapidly spreading throughout Asia. Buddhist monks would tend to and display Bonsai trees in their monasteries. Bonsai was introduced to Japan in this manner. The exact time of Bonsais arrival in Japan is debatable, however it can be estimated that by 1195 AD the art form was present.

Once the art form got to Japan, it evolved to new heights. Initially, the trees would only be seen in monasteries, but overtime it became a symbol of prestige and honor. This meant everyone from aristocrats to ordinary peasant people grew some form of a tree in a pot. The ideals and philosophy of Bonsai continued to change and evolve over the years. For the Japanese, Bonsai represents a blend of ancient beliefs with the unity between nature, man and the soul.

Bonsai continued to grow in prestige throughout the Kamakura period. It was seen as an elegant practice and a highly refined art form. We can see the evolution of Bonsai in Japanese art works and scrolls. Pots with dwarf trees are found in many paintings and drawings of the time. The upper class accepted and admired the process and it became intertwined with Japanese life. This grew to a point where Bonsai were brought inside homes for display at special times. Just as we display a painting in a home with a beautiful matching frame the same was being done with Bonsai. The 'Japanese elite' would display the trees on specially designed shelves. The practices of pruning and training the plants was not yet happening, but the art was no longer reserved just for just outdoors.

THE 17TH & 18 CENTURY

Japanese arts gained great popularity during this time and was regarded highly. Bonsai was one of the arts viewed at the forefront. The art was more refined and had an almost minimalistic touch. The main factor in maintenance was removing everything besides the essentials. Only the most important parts of the plant were kept, the rest was carefully and artistically removed. These minimalistic ideals can be mirrored with the Japanese philosophy of the time. The reduction of everything to just the essential elements.

Throughout the middle of the 17th and 18th centuries Bonsai also transitioned more from an art reserved for the higher class to commonplace for the general Japanese public. This led to a greater increase in demand for the small trees. More and more dwarf trees were being collected from the wild. The increase led to establishing the art form deeper within Japanese culture and traditions.

EVOLUTION OF STYLES

Bonsai artists began experimenting with different styles. A creative freedom started to emerge and Bonsai began to vary immensely in looks. The connection between nature, man, and soul was still present, however, it was simply expanded on. Artists would introduce other culturally important elements in their plants such as rocks, and different landscapes.

The freedom created the arts known as *'bon-kei'* and '*sei-kei*'.

Bon-kei meant creating a scene around a Bonsai plant with small buildings and even people.

Sei-kei meant an artist would duplicate a landscape they had seen in miniature form around a Bonsai plant.

MID-19TH CENTURY

This is when Japan opened up to the rest of the world. Japan had been living in global isolation for over 230 years and now travelers from all over the globe could marvel at the country's traditions and treasures. Word spread quickly to the western world of interesting miniature trees in ceramic pots. Art exhibitions in Europe picked up on Bonsai and from there it became a globally recognized craft.

A great upsurge of demand began as the art was now globally popular. The Japanese could capitalize on the growing interest quickly. There was a lack naturally forming Bonsai plants thus commercial production began. Artists would train young plants to grow to look like Bonsai. Growing techniques were refined and developed with the help of wire and bamboo skewers. Nurseries were opened dedicated only to growing, training and exporting Bonsai trees. Basic styles were adopted, and this streamlined the operation.

Different areas of the world have different climates and conditions. So different plants were being used for the art to be sustainable worldwide. This global expansion and variety of plants has further evolved the Bonsai art form. Bonsai techniques have continued to develop, and it is possible to see different styles depending on country and culture. The Japanese native species for Bonsai are pines, maples and azaleas. These are regarded as the traditional Bonsai plants. In other countries figs, oaks, elms and many other species are being used.

TODAY

Today Bonsai is globally recognized as a symbol of Japanese culture and ideas. It is deeply rooted in life as it is a staple display piece during holidays and special events. As I mentioned above Bonsai used to be reserved more for the upper class. Today it is an art form enjoyed and shared by the entire population.

The evolution of Bonsai shows a long history of man and nature. The art forms global spread shows just how small the world has gotten...

In China & Japan there are bonsai that are more than 1000 years old...

-*Bonsai Facts by Verdissimo*-

2

BONSAI STYLES

There are lots of Bonsai styles, and we will do a deep dive into 5 of the more basic styles individually. First however, I want to clarify that there is no "correct" style. Bonsai art is meant to represent and mimic a tree in nature. Crafting a masterpiece is all about how *you* see the art. All styles are open to personal creativity and interpretations. The styles are only meant to get a basic understanding of the art form and use as possible guidelines.

You should try to make your Bonsai tree look as natural as possible. This can only be accomplished by working with the plant. Let me clarify. If your plant has some specific characteristics; it bends to the left for example, allow it to bend that way. I recommend for you to let the tree give you "suggestions". Work with it to make its natural characteristics a beautiful feature of your Bonsai. 'Listening' to your tree will allow you to make a natural, inspiring creation.

After examining your Bonsai tree, you may find that it fits a style well or even several styles. This is part of the beauty of the art. No plant will be the same, and more often than not you can train a tree into several styles. You are working with a living plant. Even if it initially stands upright (like a *beech)* or is elegantly smooth and slender (like a *maple*) we can still interpret it to fit a variety of styles.

Overtime your eye will instinctively see different natural patterns. This will allow you to work with your plant and train it to grow in a clean, purposeful way. Stick through the growing phases (... and maybe some pains) and you will get rewarded.

The 5 Bonsai styles we will look into are the following: upright, informal upright, cascade, semi-cascade, and slanting/windswept. I did not rank them from best to worst style, as there is no such thing. Each form has its own individual beauty, serenity and is open to different interpretations.

FORMAL UPRIGHT (CHOKKAN)

Formal Upright - Image source: Creative Commons, Author: Neitram, Editor: Simon Eugster, 20 July 2006

The *upright* style is a commonly seen form of Bonsai. It is the natural growth that occurs when a tree grows under perfect conditions. This means the plant is exposed to plenty of light and does not have any competing trees surrounding it. The main element of this style is a perfectly straight trunk that naturally and evenly tapers off from base to apex. This means the trunk is thicker at the bottom and gets progressively thinner up to its peak. The tree's branches in *upright* style should be symmetrical and evenly spaced, so the tree looks very balanced. It is a challenging style to produce.

The species of trees I can recommend for this style are:

- Pines
- Spruces
- Junipers

These plants naturally follow the characteristics mentioned before.

To achieve this style properly branching should begin at about 1/3rd to 1/4th of the total length of the trunk. This makes the bottom thickest section of the trunk visible from the front. It is common for the placement of branches to follow a pattern. The first branch up from the bottom is the longest and to keep things proportionate is trained to grow to about 1/3rd of the total height of the tree. Your goal is to also have this first branch growing at a 90-degree angle. This will be the longest and the 'heaviest' of the branches featured on your Bonsai.

As we "climb" higher up our Bonsai we will find our second branch. The second branch directly counters the first, it is just situated slightly higher up on the trunk. This somewhat staircase like pattern continues up to the top of our plant. As the branch structure rises they shorten, and the tree develops a cone or spear like form.

The top of a "formal upright" Bonsai style is generally thick with leafage. This makes it hard to see deeper into the top of the tree and figure out its internal structure at its peak. As I mentioned above, the main characteristic of this style is a straight trunk. At its peak however, there should be a branch. This is accomplished by cutting off the growing tip of the trunk with each new year and wiring a new branch in position at the top. Now a branch will form the apex of the Bonsai. This is a difficult task to complete, but it produces gorgeous results when accomplished properly.

INFORMAL UPRIGHT (MOYOGI)

Informal Upright - Image source: Creative Commons, Author: Neitram, Editor: Simon Eugster, 20 July 2006

The *informal upright* style is another commonly seen in Bonsai art. The style is also a common occurrence in nature. Trees will bend or alter their direction in an 'S' shape depending on many factors including wind, other trees/buildings, shade or movement towards light. In an informal upright the plants trunk should bend slightly either to the left or right.

> <u>Brother's green note</u>: *In the Bonsai art form a tree's trunk should never bend towards the viewer. A Bonsai should be displayed in a way that it is possible to view its curvy characteristics (...if it has them).*

The species of trees I can recommend for this style are:

- Japanese maple
- Trident maple
- Conifers
- Ornamental trees

For dramatic results consider at:

- Pomegranate & other flowering trees

An informal upright Bonsai follows many of the same basic principles of a formal upright Bonsai it is just simply (you guessed it...) *informal*. The plants trunk still grows in a tapering fashion, however the direction and branch positioning is more off. It demonstrates *informal*ities that would occur to a tree that was exposed to a variety of elements from an earlier age. The trunk grows with a curve or in a twisting manner with branches strategically positioned to counterbalance the effects. It is common for at every turn or twist to be branching.

The crown of an "informal upright" Bonsai is similarly to a "formal upright" Bonsai thick with foliage. The beauty of this style is that although the tree is curved or features a series of curves, its apex is always located directly above the base of the tree.

CASCADE (KENGAI)

Cascade - Image source: Creative Commons, Author: Neitram, Editor: Simon Eugster, 20 July 2006

This is a very interesting Bonsai style. The tip of a

cascade style Bonsai will reach below the base of its pot or container. To some it may seem strange but this is a normal occurrence in nature. A tree where its tip grows below its base? This happens when a tree grows on a steep cliff, it can bend downwards depending on many factors (light, rocks or snow and a variety of other reasons). A Bonsai in this style shows the battle of nature versus gravity. The trunk naturally tapers similarly to the styles I mentioned before, just that it grows downward. The plants branches will still grow facing upward, seeking the light. This style truly reflects the shape of a tree that has had a hard time growing but persists and succeeds.

The species of trees I can recommend for this style are:

- Junipers (Chinese, Green mound, Needle, Japanese garden)
- Pines (Japanese black & white, Scotch, Mountain)

There are many other types of trees that can be used for this style of Bonsai. It is simply important to make sure the tree isn't naturally straight or upright. Trying to coax a naturally straight trunk tree into downward growth will not produce the look we want in this style.

It is challenging to maintain a downward growing tree with Bonsai. All trees have a natural tendency to grow upwards toward light. It takes a lot of careful wiring and anchoring. If this is done right, the cascade style is incredibly pleasing to admire. It has a very elegant free flowing look. Although the plant is growing downwards its branches spread out evenly or alternating and give the Bonsai a balanced look.

The cascade style would not be complete without the tree being situated in a tall narrow pot. This enhances the style and creates an overall more dramatic look.

SEMI-CASCADE (KAN-KENGAI)

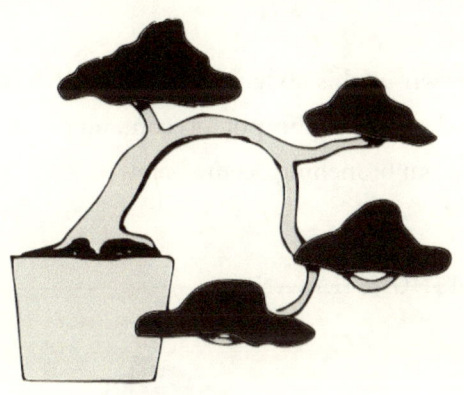

Semi- Cascade - Image source: Creative Commons, Author: Neitram, Editor: Simon Eugster, 20 July 2006

The semi-cascade style is almost identical to the cascade Bonsai style. The only difference is that the tip of the plant does not drop below its base. A semi-cascade is found on cliffs in nature just like the cascade style but it is also commonly found on river banks and lakes. This style of Bonsai is regarded by many as the essence of beauty in the art. However, as I mentioned before, it all comes down to personal preference. There is no 'best' style.

The species of trees I can recommend for this style are:

- Flowering cherry trees
- Junipers

- Cedars

The crown in this style of Bonsai usually ends just above the rim of the pot or container. The plants subsequent branching occurs below.

SLANTING (SHAKAN)

Slanting - Image source: Creative Commons, Author: Neitram, Editor: Simon Eugster, 20 July 2006

It is easy to understand why this Bonsai style is called *slanting* style. It features a plant that leans in one direction. This occurs in nature when a tree grows in conditions with heavy winds or deep shade.

A tree's trunk in this style can be straight or curved, it simply needs to lean in a direction. It is important for the plants roots are deep and well developed. Especially on the side counter to the direction it leans. This allows the tree to be supported properly. It can add up to a lot of weight for the roots to uphold and reinforce.

I can recommend almost any tree for this style of Bonsai as it is quite simple. These trees will do great:

- Maples
- Pines
- Japanese Ceders

The first branch will grow on the opposite side of the direction the tree is leaning in. This creates the sense of a better counterbalance. Slanting Bonsai have many of the same characteristics of a formal & informal upright Bonsai. The plants trunk can be bent or straight but it will taper off towards the top. Its main characteristic is the *'slant'* of the trunk to the left or right. The trees apex will never curl back to be directly over the base of the Bonsai.

You can achieve this look quite simply with your Bonsai, but there are many ways to go about it. While your plant is young, it can easily be trained to angle.

This is accomplished by wiring the trunk until it is in position. We will explore wiring in more detail in chapters 10 and 11.

Another creative technique that is commonly used to achieve this style is by placing the Bonsai's pot or container at a slant. This will cause the tree to still naturally grow upwards. Then when the pot is put down again in its traditional position, the tree will be slanted in a direction.

The branches in this style will look best if their leafage grows upward, and not towards the leaning trunk. Some masters find that having the branches grow slightly downward is also more visually appealing.

... EVEN MORE STYLES!

We just explored the 5 basic styles of Bonsai. Over the years many of them have advanced and created new styles. They all still resemble and mimic scenes that can be found in nature. Although they are technically their own style most of them can be traced back to a varying form of what we explored above.

❝

The object is not to make the tree look like a bonsai, but to make the bonsai look like a tree.

-John Naka-

3

INDOOR OR OUTDOOR

You may be thinking, trees are usually found outside... correct? True, and Bonsai is generally thought of as an outdoor art. However, art can be beautifully displayed outside and *inside*. Bonsai is the miniaturization of trees and they can be seen as plants in a pot which are often found inside homes. The opinions of where to garden Bonsai vary...

Truthfully there is no right answer. Although you will see much better results growing a Bonsai outside rather than inside, it is technically possible to keep it indoors. Depending on the species of tree it will probably not flourish the same way but it will not die.

It is important to recognize that you are growing and developing an actual tree. It may have some characteristics of a houseplant but it still needs the same care as a tree. They need lots of sunlight, good air circulation and optimal humidity levels. Many tree species also need to go through a variety of seasonal changes to grow properly. They need to go through Fall, Spring and a cold winter. This is very difficult to replicate in our homes. Inside a Bonsai will receive much less light, the air is dryer and still, humidity levels are lower and your tree will never experience winter. This last point is crucial as most species must go dormant for some months. Without this cold winter it will never flourish as well as it could.

Bonsai that were cultivated outdoors can be temporarily displayed inside. It is rare for an outdoor species to die right away when left to grow inside. It can survive indoors for months and some even for years. The trees health will slowly start to go downhill and this makes them susceptible to diseases. It can be compared to when our immune system slowly disappears. Simple diseases can have grave consequences. The same can be said for Bonsai... the tree becomes prone to bugs and disease. Slowly the tree will display signs of poor health (yellowing & losing of leaves) and slowly die.

There are some species of tree that will tolerate indoor conditions. They need a lot of attention and care taking. It is important to have the correct placement in your home. There is also a minority of species that would not survive a winter outdoors.

These are mostly tropical and subtropical varieties that can't handle temperatures below 50 - 40 degrees Fahrenheit. This means they **must** be inside if you live in somewhere that faces a cold winter. For temperatures above 50 degrees Fahrenheit the plants can be left outside.

Plants that do well as indoor Bonsai include the following:

- Aralia
- Azalea
- Norfolk Pine
- Ficus
- Boxwood
- Gardenia
- Serissa

---

*The Brothers Green Note: All of the plants mentioned above can be wired to help direct them during growth. They are all woody stemmed plants.

When growing a Bonsai indoors, I recommend using grow lights. 12 hours of light under those works well. During the summer months it is best to leave a Bonsai outside, situated in partial shade.

There is no coniferous species of tree that is able to survive indoor growing for over 2 - 3 years. Conifers are woody plants, and mostly trees that are found all over the world. Most Bonsai trees are of the coniferous species.

In mild climates it is best for most Bonsai to remain outside. The more temperate climate plants will need winter protection. After they are given the required time they need to be dormant, it is better to bring them indoors. This way you won't have to worry about the plant dying and they are able to continue growing in perfect conditions.

Most beginners are very excited about the possibilities of keeping their Bonsai indoors. I recommend you to first start with developing your skills and growing your plant(s) outdoors. Eventually you will be experienced enough to grow and display your art indoors at all times but this takes time.

The earth says much to those who listen...

 ———————— *-Rumi-* ————————

4

TOOL BOX

Creating a Bonsai masterpiece takes a lot of work. There is the caring for the plant itself, style, growing and shaping and then there is that adding of details. With all of this work comes the need for the correct tools.

Just as the plant takes on a very minimalistic look there is also only a need for a minimal amount of tools. The tools simply make certain jobs easier and quicker to complete. They vary in price from a few to dollars to a few hundred dollars. I recommend for you not to spend a fortune on your tools and to get a basic set at a price you can afford. Overtime you can see if you need a more advanced set or if extra tools are necessary. With proper care and use, your tools will last you a lifetime.

Below I will go into detail, exploring some of the

basic tools you can consider purchasing.

CONCAVE CUTTERS

This is one of the most important tools you can have in the art. These cutters allow you to clean up your tree from excessive branching. Concave cutters also leave behind a very interesting wound when a branch is removed. These cuts callous over in an almost spotless way. The cut also heals quickly, and so it becomes almost impossible to see that a cut was ever made. This tool will truly enhance your art and so is an essential part of your collection.

SCISSORS/PRUNING SHEARS

Scissors are a necessary tool for doing fine work in a small space. Trust me, there will be plenty of fine work to do in small spaces when it comes to Bonsai. It is best when the scissors are very sharp and it would be optimal to only use them for Bonsai work. At first a small set of pruning shears may be sufficient but eventually you will want to move to a dedicated pair of scissors or shears.

WIRE & WIRE CUTTERS

Wire cutters won't have to be your most urgent purchase. You will eventually wire your plant and this means you will need to remove it at some point. Wire cutters will make this an easier process. They will help you cut the wiring without harming your tree. Although you won't need them right away, they will be an essential tool at a later point.

You will also want to have plenty of wire as a part of your collection. It is best to get anodized copper wire in several thicknesses. This style of wire is very flexible and malleable so you can properly shape your Bonsai. Then when bent and positioned properly, the wire will set and hold firmly. I will explain wiring in more detail in chapter 10 but you will use it to position and train branches.

TWEEZERS

Tweezers are very useful for grooming in Bonsai. You can use them to pinch back some new growth and remove some of the smaller unwanted items from your plant. Tweezers are great for those clearing up those minor details.

KNOB CUTTERS

Knob cutters and concave cutters perform in almost the same fashion. The only difference is that knob cutters feature a spherical head. This means instead of leaving no evidence behind when cutting a branch it leaves behind a small hollowed out scar. This can be useful when you want to portray aging or other visual features to your tree.

SMALL/FOLDING SAW

Owning a miniature tree calls for owning a miniature saw. It isn't always necessary but it will be useful to have one of these in your collection. Branches can get larger than the diameter of your cutters, and then a saw becomes very useful. Keep in mind that over time your Bonsai will increase in size.

ROOT RAKE

A root rake is used to clear dirt from the roots of your tree. It is most common to use this tool while you are repotting you Bonsai. It assists in gently combing out the plants roots and removing dirt.

This would be the extent of tools I recommend all Bonsai owners to have. Some items on this list are not necessary but can prove to be very useful depending on situation.

The bonsai is not you working on the tree; you have to have the tree work on you.

-John Naka-

GROW FROM SEEDS OR BUY A TREE?

I often get asked "Do you grow your Bonsai trees from seeds?" This is a great question, and while it is possible to start your Bonsai from seed, it would take a very long time to see the fruits of your labor. Technically, if you were to start your Bonsai journey at around age 4, it would be fine to start with just a plants seed. In general, I recommend starting your hobby with a young sapling.

Seeds take quite a while to germinate and become a plant suitable for Bonsai. A tree will need to have around a trunk the diameter of half an inch to an inch. The time this takes is variable, it depends on the species of the tree.

Bonsai trees are not very different from the trees you see around you everyday outside. Although they are miniature in comparison, they live and continue to grow just as long as their 'parent' trees (Over hundreds of years, and some species over thousands of years). That gives a plant a lot of time to grow. So I recommend people to not wait years for a seed to grow but to get some faster satisfaction out of the hobby by purchasing a sapling. Your skills will develop faster and your love for the art will grow faster as well.

As long as a plant has a relatively thick trunk it has good Bonsai potential. You can visit your local nursery or garden store and explore what they have to offer there. I am always positively surprised when I go to my local shop to find some great low priced deals on potential plants. Training these plants with pruning and wiring will deliver beautiful Bonsai. Other often passed up opportunities for Bonsai include plants in your garden or nearby woods. Often there are great plants surrounding us.

As general advice, I recommend selecting plant specimen tolerant of being handled. Meaning they are forgiving to being cut, wired and replanted. Some trees I recommend that can easily be found (depending on area) are:

- Lonicera
- Juniperus
- Cotoneasters
- Maples

... Depending on your area there are many more.

Getting a tree native of the area you live in will make creating your Bonsai masterpiece much simpler and just as rewarding. You won't have to recreate the plants living conditions, and your care will allow it to flourish.

The best time to plant a tree was 20 years ago. The second best time is now.

-*Chinese Proverb*-

6

TREE SPECIES

DIFFERENT POPULAR BONSAI TREES TO CONSIDER

So far I have recommended some tree species to look into for specific Bonsai styles. In this section I want to dive a little deeper into some of the more popular species amongst Bonsai enthusiasts. I have listed the species and provided some general information along with growing tips. They are all quite 'forgiving' trees that are suitable for beginners. This is important as you need to be able to make learning mistakes.

Enjoy the list below.

Beech

Beech trees are perfect for Bonsai art. They are commonly found throughout the worlds temperate zones which means they are accustomed to facing various seasons.

Common Style(s):

- Informal styles

Soil:

- Will do well in an alkaline (lime) soil

Tips:

I recommend trimming leaves every other year in order to reduce the size of leaves on larger types. It is best to trim as early as possible because it is common for beech trees to leaf only once for a short time every year.

Cedar

There are many trees all over the world named cedars. There are a variety of types.

Common Style(s):

- Upright, cascade, slanting

Soil:

- Will do well in open, grittier soil

Tips:

Cedars used in Bonsai usually have weaker root systems. In nature this is not as big of a problem because they are able to reach their roots deeper in the earth. In a pot this is more challenging. The roots are also sensitive to frost, so during a harsher winter it is best to keep these plants sheltered.

Cherry

Cherry trees are a member of the 'rosaceous' family. This family of species in very diverse and it includes cherry trees, pears, apples, roses, strawberries and a couple others. The Cherry family itself is also quite diverse featuring plums, peaches, and apricots. All the cherry family members make excellent Bonsai.

Common Style(s):

- It is suitable for pretty much every Bonsai style.

Soil:

- Simple, any (organic) potting soil

Tips:

It is best to keep a cherry trees soil moist at all times. I also recommend for you to prune the tree regularly. This will stimulate healthy stem-and-leaf production.

Elm

Elm trees are some of the most beginner friendly trees available. They will 'forgive' you for almost anything and they are very durable. They grow in a variety of soils and should be readily available in your area.

An Elm tree is a plant where I find there is potential to grow it from a seed. It will still take a lot of patience, and it will not produce results for a long time. However, since its seed germinates fast, you will eventually have a beautiful work of art.

Cedar Elm

Cedar elms are great for beginners and they are usually easy to obtain. They do well in most soil types and need little water maintenance. They prefer to be kept in slightly dryer conditions.

Chinese Elm

Chinese elms are potential plants that can potentially thrive indoors. They have a predictable growth pattern and like most elms are very 'forgiving'. This is another beginner friendly Bonsai. The bark of a Chinese elm is very interesting. It can vary from smooth to cork like, and features many traits. It's potential to thrive indoors stems from the fact that it can be kept and thrive in the shade and full sun. It is just important to keep an eye on it so that it doesn't dry out.

Common Style(s):

- Can be pruned and shaped to any style.

Soil:

- Simple, any (organic) potting soil

Tips:

Elms respond very well to getting their leaves trimmed. There can even be some years where it will be suitable to trim twice. Growth will occur quickly.

Ginkgo

Ginkgo trees were initially thought to be extinct until some living specimen were discovered in China. The trees are sexual, meaning they are either male or female.

Common Style(s):

- Formal & Informal uprights

Soil:

- A standard soil type is great, but it must drain well.

Tips:

Ginkgos are great Bonsai plants however they are quite difficult to style. This is a tree type that is best left alone mostly, so it can take on its own shape. Ginkgos also feature soft roots so just like a ceder tree it will need protection over winter.

Camellia

Camellia trees are a very popular Bonsai. They show off an array of flowers and when refined; they are some of the most beautiful pieces of art.

Common Style(s):

- Informal upright, with single or multiple trunks. They can also be shaped into the cascade style.

Soil:

- They are acid-loving plants, so it is best to use an acidic humus-rich soil.

Tips:

Camellias perform best when they are placed partially in the shade. They will also need some protection from frost.

Dwarf Pomegranate

Dwarf pomegranates have been gaining popularity

over the years. They have great flowering and fruiting characteristics. This combined with a unique twisting style trunk makes it a very sought after species. This style trunk allows for old age to appear naturally and more easily.

Common Style(s):

- Informal upright, cascade, and various landscape style combining rocks.

Soil:

- A mixture of lime and sand is perfect soil for them.

Tips:

Dwarf Pomegranates enjoy Mediterranean climates and conditions. They need it to stay hot and sunny. Although it thrives in the sun, it will need plenty of water.

Ficus

A ficus tree is popular to have in the house. Fake ficus trees are often created and displayed in offices and homes. As a Bonsai it is a beautiful piece. Often referred to as a 'rainforest fig' it can naturally be found in Southeast Asia. In the wild the plant will fruit every year however as a Bonsai this is a rare occurrence.

Common Style(s):

- A lot of enthusiasts combine these trees with rocks in various styles.

Soil:

- Humus-rich, well-drained soil will keep these guys happy and healthy.

Tips:

Ficus trees love to be in the sun and do not thrive as well in the cold. They will need shelter from cold winds. Its roots are also quite brittle at first but when it is more developed they gain a lot of strength and become one of the more powerful areas of this tree.

Japanese Black Pine

These trees are the epitome of Bonsai as an art. They are not for beginners and take many years of care and attention to achieve its masterful look. Deciding to cultivate one of these is a big task. A black pine naturally has all of the opposite characteristics that are looked for in a Bonsai. The cone shape look we strive for is not something this plant naturally looks to perform. Its upper branches usually get most of its energy and this leaves the lower branches in a weaker position.

Common Style(s):

- It can be grown into any style outside of the broom.

Soil:

- A sandy clay soil is best for the black pine.

Tips:

A black pine should be developed outdoors and it enjoys full sun. It can thrive in very hot temperatures. One thing of note is that the trees soil should dry out in between watering.

Trees are poems that the earth writes upon the sky.

-Khalil Gibran-

7

WHAT TO LOOK FOR IN A TREE

It is essential for your plant or tree to have specific qualities to ensure that it will make a good Bonsai. In this section we will explore some things you should look for when getting a sapling.

I have narrowed it down to 5 main points to consider when looking for a potential Bonsai plant in a nursery or garden center.

1. THE ROOTS

Strong and healthy roots are key when considering a plant to use for Bonsai. Have a good look at a tree's base and roots to make sure it appears to have a strong foundation. It is best when the plants base appears to spread out gently in a radial pattern. The foundation should provide stability and also invite a viewers eyes up from the base to explore the rest of the tree. An unstable looking plant will make it harder to create a well-balanced, beautiful Bonsai.

2. THE TRUNK

We are now slowly making up way up from the base of the tree to its midsection. The trunk is very important to examine and the qualities to look out for differ depending on the style of the plant. Usually, a thick, stable base which tapers gently as it increases in height will make for a suitable tree. If you are considering a *formal upright* style Bonsai, then it is important for the plant to have a very straight trunk. If you are thinking about going with other styles, then some curvature and other "moves" in the trunk are important to examine.

I recommend looking for a trunk that curves in unusual and interesting ways. This often results in a very rewarding Bonsai. The unique movements will invite a viewer to examine the plant further. When looking for curvature in a potential plant follow the main trunk like to its highest point. This will tell you a lot about how the tree will naturally be willing to twist and bend.

3. BRANCHING PATTERN

Observing proper branching is a little more difficult to master. Most garden centers and nurseries do not have trained Bonsai plants, so you will have to do some research. If you notice a tree having thick lower branches and thinner higher ones, you may have found a suitable match. These would be the branches that form the main structure of your Bonsai. The plant should also only have small leaves. If the leaves are overly large, it will result in a Bonsai that looks out of proportion. At times it can be a little difficult to see the right fit and balance of branches with the tree's trunk. If you do not feel that you see the right branching pattern move on and keep searching. You will feel it when you have found the right tree to work with.

When you spot a branching pattern that speaks to you a certain style for your Bonsai will also come to vision. You will see the potential for a *slanting style,* or a cascade. You will see where it still needs some growth, support, branches and how it can flower. The Bonsai artist in you will observe how you can work with it to bring out its beauty.

4. HEALTH

A step that definitely cannot be skipped is examining the plant for good health. For your first couple of Bonsai plants it is better to skip on a plant you are not 100 percent confident in or sure of. If you are not convinced the tree is healthy then move on to the next one. It will need to be strong enough to handle your experimenting with wiring, pruning and potting.

For examining health I recommend that you remove the plant from its container. This way you can better check that everything is in good shape. Observe if there are any white fibrous roots (this is a positive sign for good health and growth) around its soil. Consider the following:

- Is there new growth?

- Does it have colorful and vibrant leaves?

- Does the plants soil look good and hydrated enough?

- Does the plant look healthy overall?

5. AGING POTENTIAL

The final step to consider when picking out a tree is its potential for having an aged look. In Bonsai it is very important for a tree to look old. This aged look is primarily made possible by the tree's bark and trunk. The bark should have an attractive look and the trunk should have good girth. What also gives the appearance of more age is having some of the tree's root structure above soil. Having about 1/3rd of the tree's roots exposed will create a beautiful dramatic scene perfect for Bonsai.

Considering the 5 points above will allow you to select a great sapling to start your Bonsai journey. It will have a harmonious arrangement roots, branching, bark, a solid trunk and great health. Keep in mind the importance of balance and aging potential and there you have the foundations for a beautiful Bonsai.

All our wisdom is stored in the trees...

   ─ *-Santosh Kalwar-*

8

PLANTING A TREE IN A POT

Bonsai trees are grown and developed in a pot or container. So part of planting a Bonsai is selecting the right container. It is important for the pot to harmonize with the plant. We will dive deeper into this subject in chapter 13 (repotting). Take your time to find the right container but also realize that you will be able to change it if you are no longer satisfied with the overall look of your Bonsai. The decision is not set in stone, so have fun with it and don't be afraid of being creative. The first containers for Bonsai plants are called training pots. These pots are for developing the tree and assist it in recovering from getting its roots pruned. Anything that can hold heavy roots will do well as a training pot. I find it best however, to develop it in a container that looks similar to its eventual display pot.

It is common practice for a Bonsai tree to be positioned off-center in its pot. This is important to add some asymmetrical value to the completed piece, but it also has a deeper symbolic meaning. It is believed that the center of a container is where heaven and earth meet, and nothing else should be placed there to interrupt this.

Before placing a Bonsai in it's growing container it is important to use the correct soil matter to plant your tree. The growing container should also feature some draining holes. These holes should be at least half an inch in diameter. This prevents your plant from 'drowning' when you water it. When these basics are covered it now becomes important to prepare the training pot. Cut pieces of mesh that are slightly bigger than each of the draining holes your pot has. Next, secure the pieces of mesh with some wire so they stay in place. The mesh is in place so that soil does not disappear out of the pot as you water your tree.

After completing those steps it is time to secure your trees roots to the pot. This is done by taking a longer piece of wire and entering it from the bottom of your pots draining holes. This wire is called an 'anchorage wire'. You will attach it to the roots of your tree. After it is attached and secure, you can continue filling up the pot with the appropriate soil. Pat it all down and water it a bit to make sure everything is draining properly. Some enthusiasts enjoy adding some touches to their Bonsai at this point. They add moss, other plants or rocks around their tree to recreate a fully sized tree in the wild.

Traditional Bonsai pots are available in a variety of shapes. Online and at some specialized shops they can be found in round, oval, square, rectangular and hexagonal formats. It is important for the pot to compliment the Bonsai and not be too big and "loud". The viewer's eyes should be drawn to the plant itself, not the container. I do recommend using colors that complement the tree. It is fine to use a brightly colored pot for a flowering tree or one that has beautiful fall leaves. Also, if the bark on your tree is very rough or has a very textured look, try to mimic this texture on the pot. This way they compliment each other perfectly.

Brothers Green Tips:

Cascading Plants - I recommend you to use a deep pot for training a cascade plant. Eventually when it had the time to develop properly, it ends up in a shallow pot. This is common for tall specimen, they 'train' in deeper pots and then transfer to a shallow container. Cascade and semi-cascade styles of Bonsai are often found in round or rectangular pots. I feel like they look very good in those pots however, it all comes down to personal taste.

Be not afraid of growing slowly; be afraid only of standing still.

-Chinese Proverb-

9

PRUNING AND TRIMMING

Trimming and pruning your tree is how it is kept small. It 'cleans' up your Bonsai and keeps everything minimalistic leaving just the essentials. The process involves the systematic removal of the intense growth which occurs in the spring. It is key to remember however, that the new growth should not be removed all at once. This greatly damages the tree and if not done in a controlled way can cause it to die. Roots and foliage are also trimmed during this period.

People often believe that they need to be pruning and trimming their Bonsai every day. This couldn't be farther from the truth. Pruning and trimming should happen at the most 3 times a year. Bonsai can be trimmed at the start of spring, end of summer and if necessary late in the fall.

Have a look at the section below to find out what should be pruned, trimmed and nipped...

Pruning:

It is common to have to do quite some pruning to a plant you got from a garden center or nursery. Although there is plenty to disperse of, don't cut too far back so that it weakens main branches. Only excess leafage and unwanted limbs should be removed. All stubs should be left smooth with stems.

The aim of pruning your tree is to have it look just like a mature tree you would find in nature. It is quite a mindful activity; it differs greatly from shearing a hedge for example. You need to make sure the tree still has enough leaves for photosynthesis and that it can continue developing. Keep branches that are growing opposite of each other and grow towards empty/non-busy space.

Pruning maintains the right shape of a Bonsai by getting rid of all excess growth. It is also a process that encourages new growth. Some plants are more durable and respond very well to the process. They can recover well and grow healthier and faster. It all depends on the species as others will find it harder to recover. When these plants are pruned during the wrong time of year or too often, it becomes difficult for them to survive.

A common form of pruning Bonsai trees is called *finger pruning*.

This simply means pinching back new growth that doesn't align with the general shape of the plant. It encourages new bushy leaves to grow, and it makes the tree look older. Finger pruning is done with... you guessed it... your fingers. You take the unwanted growth between your thumb and forefinger, and carefully pinch it away in a twisting movement. It is better to do it carefully with your fingers as using scissors often leaves an unnatural look.

Another style of pruning is called *leaf pruning* (defoliation).

This style of pruning in Bonsai is often seen with deciduous and tropical plants. It is a way to remove excess leaves which in turn speeds up growth. By removing the leaves during a plants growing season will automatically stimulate a new growing season.

A Bonsai will only go through a thorough pruning process once in its life. A basic form is set, and then it will only have to go through more minor trimming and nipping.

. . .

Nipping:

Nipping allows you to control new growth and to further shape your plant. It also will stimulate further growth. Well-timed nips will allow a tree to develop thicker healthy new foliage. You can also control the appearance of your plants trunk. It is important to remove tiny spurs that show up before they become big enough to leave a scar.

Trimming:

Roots will also need to be trimmed throughout your Bonsai's life. There is a loose rule that there is an equal number of branches to roots ratio in Bonsai. I like to try to keep all fibrous roots whenever possible and only cut the true excess ones. The surface roots should always remain intact. They play a big role in making your Bonsai appear more aged.

It is important not to mindlessly cut away at your Bonsai. Be precise and carefully consider which branches need to go and which should stay. This way the plant stays in balance and remains healthy.

Love the trees until their leaves fall off, then encourage them to try again next year.

-Chad Sugg-

10

WIRING

After your plant is pruned another way to style and shape it, is through wiring. Most of the beautifully designed Bonsai you see have been wired at some point. It is an important part of developing in the art form. I have to be honest and say it's not the easiest task to master. For some it comes as second nature, but for most it takes longer to grasp techniques. When done well wiring gives you better control and lets you manipulate the look of your Bonsai resulting in a beautiful work of art.

In principle, wiring simply involves coiling a wire around the limbs of a tree and then bending it into a desired position. The wire then holds the tree in the position you set. After some weeks or months the part of the plant you coiled will have 'learned' and naturally stay in the desired position you set. You can then remove the wire and the tree will continue to flourish and hold itself in its new position.

Wiring allows for straight trunks or branches to be set into more realistic positions. It is easiest to perform this task with young branches. We can wire them into downward or horizontal positions which will create the impression of a mature branch. Also, if there is a section of your Bonsai that is relatively empty, wiring allows you to move/shape branches or leaves in that area. Doing this effectively, balances out your tree and so improves its appearance.

The Process and Technique

Without wiring, enthusiasts would need to be patient and incredibly lucky to have branches and leaves growing in the direction they want. Wiring makes the art of Bonsai possible. In most cases however, you should not have to wire your tree an extensive amount. We reviewed some best practices when choosing a plant for Bonsai in chapter 7. While choosing a plant I recommend that you look for one that already has potential for a style and shape you like. This way you have already taken into account the natural form of the species. You will have a rough idea of what it can look like and you use wiring as small nudges in the right direction.

I recommend beginners to use aluminum wire. It is one of the easier wires to maneuver and play with. Eventually, you will want to consider using copper wire as it has more holding power. Copper wire is more challenging to handle, so to ease the learning process I suggest aluminum. In most cases, you will need a wire that is around 1/3rd the width of the branch or trunk you wish to bend. It's about finding the balance between a wire thin enough to be easily twisted and bent, and thick enough to hold the branch in place.

It is best when branches are somewhat mobile and flexible before you wire. This is influenced by not watering the tree the day before you plan on wiring. Wait for the soil of your Bonsai to dry out slightly. This will allow the tree to be a bit more pliable. I always tell new enthusiasts to start at the bottom of the tree and work their way up. The base serves as the 'anchor' as it is the most solid piece. Also, we do not want to damage or cut into branches so I like to use foam pads as a layer of protection. The wire should be coiled only over the foam and this way the branches are protected.

Before beginning the wiring process you can estimate the amount of wire you will need. It is common to use a wire that is a 1/3rd longer than the branch you plan on wiring. Another way, a way which I prefer, is to keep the reel of wire in my hand and snip it off when I have completely wired the branch. This way you don't need to estimate and you won't run out of wire in the middle of coiling.

The most aesthetically pleasing look is achieved when wire is applied at a 45-degree angle from a branch or stem. Depending on how it is more comfortable for you use one hand to hold on to the anchor point firmly (the base) and the other to coil the wire further down the branch. Use your thumb and first finger as possible and make a circling motion with your wrist as you move around the branch. As you navigate further up the branch, you should be able to move the hand at the anchor point further along as well. Coiled wire should not move anymore as you continue to wire the remaining parts of the branch. Branches should be bent slowly and carefully. Listen for signs of a branch cracking or splitting. If you hear signs of damage stop right away.

Some species of tree grow faster than others. This not only affects how long you will need to keep wire on your plant but it also how tightly you should coil. Fast growers should be wired a lot looser. This way you do not risk cutting into the plant and leaving unnatural marks. It is important to understand your tree. Some species will not bend when they reach a certain age. They can only be wired when their branches are still young and haven't hardened.

It is important to be decisive. When wiring a branch make sure you position it how you like and then stick with that plan. Repeatedly bending and rewiring a branch will weaken your Bonsai. It is unnecessary to risk your Bonsais health in this manner.

What happens inside the plant?

If done correctly, wiring does not damage the plant in any way. In the art of Bonsai we aim to recreate what is seen in nature. This means all the styles and shapes are ways the trees thrive in naturally.

Let's have a closer look at how a branch 'learns' and develops its new position. Wiring a tree causes small fractures under the bark of a branch. The *cambium layer* of the plant will work to repair and heal the splits in the branch. When the healing process is complete, the branch will naturally hold its new position. The same process happens in nature when a strong wind bends a tree or other factors rearrange a trees structure.

If your tree is given the appropriate time to recover peacefully, it will respond well to wiring. It will continue its healthy growth and adapt well to its new shape. If a tree is weak or unhealthy to start out with, then I do not recommend wiring. Either wait for it to gain strength and recover or start with a new plant.

Look deep into nature, and then you will understand everything better.

-Albert Einstein-

11

WHEN TO WIRE

The best time to wire a Bonsai tree is largely dependent and what kind of tree it is. A general rule is that you shouldn't wire your plant(s) during the winter. Fractures that occur during wiring need time to heal. During the cold this process does not happen as easily as trees go dormant. This can prevent the branch from healing properly and cause it to die.

Theoretically, most tree species can be wired at most times of the year given enough recovery time. Lets have a look at the best times to wire depending on tree species below...

Best time to wire - Deciduous Species

Throughout warmer climates, the best time to wire

this species is in autumn(fall) as its leaves have fallen. The tree will be 'naked' which makes it easier to get a complete view of its shape. It will also still have just enough time to heal before it goes dormant for the winter.

Another great time to wire deciduous trees is in the spring right before its leaves open. You must be very careful wiring your tree around this time. New leaves and flower buds are getting ready to spring out so take care that they do not get dislodged.

Throughout the growing season deciduous trees can be wired any time. It just may be more difficult to plan the structure of your Bonsai as your trees leaves can be in the way. It can be very challenging to wire around the leaves and getting them caught in the wire can make the tree look unnatural. A positive of wiring during your trees growing season is that branches will heal very quickly. I recommend inspecting the wiring every few days so you can be sure wire isn't digging into the tree.

In general, I have found it best to wire when a tree is 'naked'. This way changes can be planned out more thoroughly.

Best Time to wire - Coniferous Species

Coniferous trees can be wired any time from spring

through fall. This species of tree will heal throughout winter, so you can still comfortably wire them late in fall. Wiring a coniferous tree usually takes a bit longer. You will need to leave the coiled wire on a branch longer, at times over winter. If temperatures drop below 15 degrees Fahrenheit, I recommend frost protection.

Coniferous species commonly need wiring annually. Most enthusiast also feel it is a species that needs a complete wiring of its structure at some point. They need to most work done to have a successful design. The best time for this is midsummer through early fall. The tree will heal fast, and you do not have to fear branches gaining a lot of thickness as they are wired.

Best time to wire - Tropical Species

These plants can be wired at almost any time of the year. They have no dormant period and there is no need to have concerns over frost. I recommend for you to check your wiring a lot with this species. Tropical trees can experience intense growth so if not checked regularly wire scarring is a high risk.

Wire can usually be removed after half a year of

'training'. Branches should remain in that position on their own. When removing the wire it is always better to cut it off carefully rather than uncoil it. Unwinding wires by hand risks breaking or snapping the branch. Wire cutters deliver the best results. If a branch happens to snap, carefully rejoin it with the help of some garden tape. It may grow back together cleanly if your tree is healthy enough.

One touch of nature makes the whole world kin.

   —William Shakespeare—

12

WATERING & FERTILIZING

Watering seems like a very simple process, but it is actually one of the most common causes of Bonsai related issues. There is a fine balance to watering your tree. Give it too little water and it will dry out and lose its health. Give it too much water and it can effectively 'drown' and rot. Lets explore some best practices for taking care of your Bonsai.

I commonly get asked by friends who are just getting started with the hobby, "what is your watering schedule?". It's a great question, but it follows the wrong train of thought. An important rule to remember is that you should never water by following a routine. Depending on species you should check for water requirements daily, however you should only water as needed. There may be a week where you have to water every day, there may also be a week where you need to water your plant only twice. Watering by following a schedule risks over-watering the plant. This eventually leads to killing your tree as its roots suffocate.

The appropriate time between watering varies on a number of factors. The tree type, humidity levels, temperature and wind all play a significant role. Some Bonsai will need to be watered every 12 hours and some every 7 days. When you notice the surface of the earth your plant is in has started to dry out, it is a sign that your tree can be watered again. It is important to note however that this depends greatly on species.

Bonsai pots are usually quite small and shallow. This limits how much a trees roots can expand and makes caring for one rather difficult. It truly shows how much care and practice enthusiasts develop for their art. Properly watering a Bonsai can be considered a skill in itself. Some trees can handle periods of dryness and others need almost constant moisture. Assessing your trees health by observing its leaves is also challenging. Many species like the Juniper do not display signs of drying until it is already too late. A Juniper can display green and healthy leaves even though its root system has died.

. . .

Fertilizer

You should fertilize your Bonsai with water soluble fertilizer twice a month throughout the growing season. The type of fertilizer depends on what kind of tree you have. I recommend you to apply the fertilizer when the soil is wet and only during or slightly before active growth. A normal houseplant fertilizer diluted to about half strength will do just fine.

Applying fertilizer is a different process from repotting, which we will check out in the next chapter...

Trees are as close to immortality as the rest of us ever come.

-Karen Joy Fowler-

13

REPOTTING

Repotting is a straightforward and simple task if carried out properly and at the right time. Most Bonsai trees will need to be repotted every year or at least every other year during spring. If they are not repotted they will eventually lose their health and their root system will suffer. It prevents the tree from becoming pot bound (*this means the plant's roots have no more room to grow anywhere*) and encourages growth of feeder roots. This makes the whole plant more efficient and healthy. During the repotting process you also replace the old soil in the pot. Over time soil becomes 'stale' and hampers growth.

You will notice that the longer you care for your Bonsai, the longer water takes to drain through the soil. This means it is time to repot your plant. Also, if the roots of your tree are crowding around the sides of the pot, it is a clear sign for you to repot.

Step 1

The first step is to remove your tree from its current pot. Do this by carefully tilting it to a side and slowly moving it out by the base of its trunk. Do not pull up too hard as you risk separating your tree from important roots. If it does not come out easily try lightly but firmly tapping the side of the pot. Another option is poking a stick through some of the drain holes to help push out the tree's roots.

Step 2

Using a hook or small rake remove any extra plants or moss and brush at the roots. Try to untangle them starting on one side and slowly working around the entire bottom. I recommend taking your time so you do not damage the plant's main roots.

Continue to shake off soil until only half of the original amount is left around the plant's roots. I recommend spraying the roots with water so they do not dry out and so that soil can be removed more easily.

. . .

Step 3

It is now time to prune the plant's roots. Use very sharp clippers as some species of trees have very stubborn root systems. Primarily cut the thick, old brown roots (They are usually the ones that were close to the edge of your pot).

Brothers Green Tip:

Make sure to wash away a lot of the soil at the location you plan on cutting roots. Cutting through roots and soil will make your scissors/clippers blunt quickly.

Step 4

After removing the old roots that are no longer efficient it is time to prune the excess thinner roots. They usually hang below the depth of the pot and need to be trimmed into a suitable shape so the plant fits comfortably in its pot again. It is perfect when your plant fits in its pot with about half an inch of space between the edges.

. . .

Step 5

You have completed the most challenging part of the repotting processes. Now it is time to clean your original pot or select a new pot. From here on out we will follow the same techniques we laid out in Chapter 8 - Planting a Tree in a Pot. We will cover the drainage holes with mesh and anchor our plant to the pot.

After the repotting process you should thoroughly water your tree. You may need to adjust soil levels as watering settles it to a lower level. Place the tree in a position where it will not have to face extreme temperatures. It needs time to recuperate properly. Also, I recommend not to add fertilizer as it can cause stress to the tree. After about a month the roots will have recovered. Enthusiasts also like to balance out all the pruning done to the roots with some pruning of branches. This way the Bonsai can recover quicker and not have to work as hard, feeding an excess of branches and leaves.

Bonsai can reach prices over $400,000...

-Bonsai Facts by Verdissimo-

14

SEASONAL CARE

Different seasons equals different ways you should take care of your Bonsai. There are different considerations and circumstances that can affect your plant. Since the trees are small, you may have to do more to protect them. Let's have a deeper look at the seasons and explore what you might need to expect...

Summer

In the summer, Bonsai from forest trees should always be outside. They need sunny days, cool nights and great ventilation. If you want to bring one inside for viewing/displaying it can only be for 3 hours maximum.

If you live in an area that does not provide this type

of summer climate you must try to recreate it. They need around 4 hours of direct sunlight every day, and then should be in the shade in the afternoon. Some enthusiasts also place their Bonsai on a slightly tilted stand. This way when it rains water can drain out of its pot more easily. Extreme conditions are never good for a Bonsai. Too much rain, sun, and wind will put your tree at risk.

Fall

During the fall it is time to prepare your Bonsai for winter. This is best done by slowing down its growth. Water the tree less frequently and do not fertilize it. I also recommend you to not prune or cut any branches after around the middle of August.

Winter

Winter is the riskiest time for a Bonsai. The consistent low temperatures and dry winds can easily kill a miniature tree. I recommend for you to protect your Bonsai when the temperature drops below 28 degrees Fahrenheit. That means placing it in a greenhouse, cold frame, or pit. These are all ways to protect your tree from frost.

If you opt for a cold frame, don't forget to water it

while it is in there. Remember to carefully assess how much water it needs. It may only be necessary every other day.

Bonsai can generally still remain outside in temperatures above 15 degrees Fahrenheit as long as they have some protection. If temperatures drop below this, it may be necessary to bring them inside. This fluctuation of environmental change is actually also not good for the tree but it may be your only option in extreme situations. Woody plants must go through a period of cold dormancy. Without this they die.

Dormancy is a trees survival strategy to stay alive over the winter. They have a biological clock that that tells the tree to prepare itself for freezing temperatures. It is something deeply rooted in its system and a step that cannot be skipped.

Throughout the winter some enthusiasts cover their Bonsai with a tarp over night, and remove it during the day. This allows the tree to remain dormant but not freeze to death.

Spring

Spring is the season of new beginnings. This is the perfect time to start new Bonsai, prune old ones and continue sharpening your skills. It is a great time to continue training your Bonsai and then let it grow and recover.

❝

The care of the Earth is our most ancient and most worthy, and after all, our most pleasing responsibility.

-Wendell Berry-

15

DISPLAYING YOUR BONSAI

After all the grooming, shaping and growing of your masterpiece there finally comes a time for showing it off. Displaying a Bonsai is a critical part of the hobby. The way your Bonsai is displayed is just as important as its style, pot and type of tree.

It is best when your Bonsai is positioned at around eye level. There is an unwritten rule that a Bonsai tree should never be placed on the ground. Also, while shaping and pruning your tree into your ideal image you pictured a front for your creation. This front side should face forward and be positioned at eye level for viewers.

As you grow your collection, you will want to consider investing in or creating a display stand. You can decide to display you work on a single stand or harmonize several pieces together on a larger bench.

It is important to remember that although you are displaying your work, it should be positioned in a way that it still gets the appropriate light or shelter from the sun it needs.

Simplicity and minimalism is key. In Japanese aesthetics and Bonsai it is essential that your tree is displayed in an uncluttered environment. This way the details can be appreciated and admired. It is the true wonder of Bonsai.

A great background for either a single Bonsai or group is a gravel bed. It doesn't take the attention away, and it allows viewers to marvel at the Bonsai. A simple table in front of a blank wall is a great fit for indoors.

I recommend for you to take your time and experiment when it comes to a display setting. Try placing it in different locations around your house (inside and outside if possible, and if the weather allows for it). You never know, a display on a window ledge or a bookshelf just might be the perfect place.

Bonsai give a room that perfect personal touch and there is a unique elegance to them. They humble viewers and show our deep connection to nature. Reading rooms, offices, entry hallways, patios and decks are all potentially great places for displaying.

I encourage you to be proud of your work and to

show it off. It is your work of art and it is an amazing statement piece of patience, dedication and care. Feel free to switch up your Bonsais display often. They can change the look and feel of the space they occupy and influence more than we realize.

Bonsais are the only trees that aren't planted to enjoy their fruit, to use their wood or to repopulate forests. Their function has become exclusively as a powerfully beautiful & relaxing decorative element.

-Bonsai Facts by Verdissimo-

16

TIPS & IDEAS!

I wanted to add a section in this book that included some overall tips and ideas. This will hopefully help beginners a lot and give seasoned enthusiasts some beneficial new ideas. Rather than create a list I let my mind flow free and the comments below are my thoughts written down. They are things I wish I knew when I first started, what I learned the hard way, and what I try to keep in mind...

... Enjoy!

... Bonsai is an art of personal preference and scope. Perfection does not exist, and you will make mistakes. This is normal and happens even to seasoned Bonsai masters...

... *Trees die.* Unfortunately, this is a sad fact of the hobby. We are working with living things and we must respect this. When this regrettably happens it is best to try to figure out and understand why. This way you learn from your mistakes and it can be prevented in the future...

... *Responsibility.* When you put a tree in a pot, you are committing yourself to caring for it. Bonsai is not simply a hobby, it carries with it a responsibility. With patience and care the rewards are tremendous...

... *Patience is key.* Nothing in Bonsai delivers immediate gratification. This is usually the case with other achievements in life as well. Talented artists, athletes, entrepreneurs usually work hard for over 10 years to be called an 'overnight' success. With your tree it may also take years before you consider it a 'Bonsai'. Don't be discouraged by this, enjoy the process and the experience...

... *Let nature do its work.* It is common for us to want to continually tinker and mess with our trees. *Just another little nip here, and little sprinkle of water here, oh and let me just prune this little section.* Follow daily requirements like checking for water and make sure your plant is in good health, but otherwise, let the tree grow. Enjoy looking at it and let nature do its work...

... Pruning and shaping is necessary but give your tree enough of a break to recover. Sometimes it is better for your tree to have some out-of-place leaves. It needs to be allowed to grow freely at times, this keeps it strong and healthy...

... *The importance of timing.* Timing is critical in the art of Bonsai. Remember not to carry out big shaping jobs or repotting at the wrong time of the year. This can lead to health issues that are hard to recover from for the tree. A Bonsai repotted at the wrong time of the year can survive and even grow a bit, but it won't flourish the same way it potentially could have...

... *Let the tree rest.* Several operations like wiring and replanting cause a plant a lot of stress. Give your tree rest in between high impact jobs. I have found that a good rule of thumb is to wait around two months between working on your Bonsai. If you see clear signs of strong growth, then this is also a sign that your tree is strong enough to work on...

... Although Bonsai are very delicate and need good care, they can also be very durable and forgiving. Making a mistake is usually not the end of the world. I have seen many trees make a strong comeback after first looking very weak...

... Some beginners get discouraged and start to believe that the hobby is too expensive, difficult and time consuming. This is simply not true, you will learn that it is relaxing, fun and liberating. Bonsai is an art and form of expression...

... There are no strict rules to Bonsai. The point is to gain enjoyment out of the hobby and you may personalize your trees style as YOU wish. Use this book, other books and videos as guides to help create your vision...

… Things will not always go according to plan. Enjoy the process and keep learning. Everyone was a beginner at one point or another…

This oak tree and me, we're made of the same stuff.

-Carl Sagan-

AFTERWORD

"Bon-sai"

The art of Bonsai can seem very daunting to beginners when they first start, but in actuality is as simple as, tray (*bon*) planting (sai). It is easy to over-complicate the practice with so many different tree species, shapes and techniques when it actually all comes down to a plant in a tray. A plant in a tray that you can uniquely style and shape. The most important aspect for a beginner is to learn how to keep your tree healthy and how to shape it.

We covered an array of topics and I want to sincerely thank you for reading this book. I am honored you picked it up and I wish you great success on your journey with the art of Bonsai.

On the last day of the world I would want to plant a tree.

-W.S. Merwin-

THANK YOU

Thank you for reading this book, I hope you enjoyed!

If you found the information provided useful, I would truly appreciate you leaving a review. Your honest opinion will make it easier for other readers to make a good purchasing decision. You will also be helping me compete with big publishing companies who have large advertising budgets and get hundreds of reviews. Thank you for your considerations and have an awesome day!

RESOURCES PAGE

Besides my own knowledge and experiences, I used the following awesome sources to create this book:

Bonsaisite. (n.d.). Retrieved from http://www.Bonsaisite.com/

Bonsai Styles. (n.d.). Retrieved from https://www.Bonsaiempire.com/origin/Bonsai-styles

Online Guide On How To Grow A Bonsai Tree. (n.d.). Retrieved from https://www.growaBonsaitree.com/

Noall, L. (2016, October 03). Potting Bonsai Trees - A Step-by-Step Guide. Retrieved from https://www.Bonsaidirect.co.uk/blog/Bonsai-care-advice/potting-guides/potting-Bonsai-trees-a-step-by-step-guide/

Potting. (n.d.). Retrieved from http://www.Bonsaicarebasics.com/potting.html

F. (2017, June 26). Bonsai Tree Care for Beginners. Retrieved from https://www.ftd.com/blog/share/Bonsai-tree-care

Bonsai Pots. (n.d.). Retrieved from https://www.Bonsaiempire.com/basics/Bonsai-care/advanced/choosing-pots

Bonsaicarebasics. (n.d.). Retrieved from http://www.Bonsaicarebasics.com/

Bonsaidirect. (n.d.). Retrieved from https://www.Bonsaidirect.co.uk/

www.ingramcontent.com/pod-product-compliance
Lightning Source LLC
LaVergne TN
LVHW040104080526
838202LV00045B/3771